POETS LAUREATE OF KENTUCKY

To: Michell and Denny Locey.

Best Wishes on the new
House.

Betty J. Sparks

Oct. 30, 2004

Poets Laureate of Kentucky

Betty J. Sparks

WIND PUBLICATIONS
2004

First edition

International Standard Book Number 1-893239-20-9
Library of Congress Control Number 2003115476

Cover Photo – "Laurel Creek" by C.G. Hughes

PREFACE

I began collecting information about the Kentucky poet laureates for my own interest. After I had collected quite a bit of material I realized others might be interested in my scrapbook. It is my intention that this book retain that scrapbook flavor.

At first, I collected information on the poet laureates I knew personally, or had met at some time, including Paul Salyers, Lee Pennington, Jim Wayne Miller, James Still, and Joy Bale Boone. With the help of friends, ads in newspapers, and the internet, I found addresses of most of the remaining poets or their family members. The only poet laureate for whom I failed to locate either a friend or family member was Edward G. Hill. At the Frankfort Capitol Annex I got a list of the names of the poets' counties and who nominated them for the post. I visited college archives, the Kentucky History Center, and libraries from Ashland to Western Kentucky State University. That was the easy part. The most difficult task in assembling the book was obtaining permission to use the poems and acquiring photographs. What at first had seemed a simple project, required more than two years to complete. My hope and prayer is that I have given a proper account of the information, with credit due to the proper persons.

I am greatly indebted to friends and family members for their advice, support and encouragement, and to Raymond Keaton for his assistance in finding addresses of poets or their family members.

For traveling with me to colleges, archives, and libraries, my thanks to Ruth (Sis) Ramey, Helen Hunt, Delores Arthur, Iva Rogers, and Cindy Clark; to Ashland Community College Librarian, Shirley Boyd, for her help with updates on poets' information, and to the families and friends of the poet laureates, my thanks. And special thanks to Michelle Polakovs for her assistance in editing.

— Betty J. Sparks

TABLE OF CONTENTS

PART III – SCRAPBOOK

INTRODUCTION

Richard Taylor

Most of us live in the world of prose, a language of commerce, information, and everyday practicality. In this necessary world bills are paid, food put on the table, understandings reached, test questions responded to, and warnings not to step from the curb or to shut off the tractor usually heeded. Poetry, language wearing its best clothes, is regarded as secondary, the medium of greeting card sentiments and the few lines we—those of who are old enough— had to memorize from Shakespeare, William Ernest Henley, Emily Dickinson, or gray-bearded Longfellow. Too often, mention of poetry is met with a wink of indulgence, expressions of perplexity, or a look of downright suspicion. It is as though poetry's subtlety and probings of the spirit have no place in a world dominated by things, by language applied at its most direct and superficial, by speakers who are expected to say what they mean without confusing inflexions, nuance, or underlying insight. Increasingly, however, both here and nationally, poetry has a growing audience as people begin to ask fundamental questions about life that TV's "Fear Factor" and the evening news don't answer. Poetry, as Ezra Pound reminds us, is news that stays news.

Though we often deny it, most of us live alternately in both worlds, the domains of prose and poetry. They are neighboring properties whose boundaries and fence-lines are uncertain, often overlapping, sometimes connected only by subterranean routes. One informs the other, enriching, provoking, interpreting the complexities of our daily experience. All of us, I am convinced, carry on throughout our lives an unspoken dialogue with ourselves as a means of coming to terms with the mystery of our presence on this planet and the miracle of life itself. If that dialogue is neglected, we are left with the unexamined life that Socrates regarded as not worth living. A good poem offers witness to this condition of being alive through language, through the phenomenon of one human giving voice to some portion of experience, the gentle and not so gentle friction of our being abroad in the world.

Good poems and poets take us places prose can't, though the corollary that prose carries us where poems can't (the internal revenue service code, for example, or a mathematical formula) also is true. As a friend put it recently, "the language of God is numbers (meaning how we quantify the physical world); the word of God (how we join that world and spirit) is poetry." "Ecstasy," as poet Lorine Neidecker tells us, "can't be constant." No, but ecstasy, wisdom, and insight into the world of spirit and higher feeling enter through the doors of perception that poetry opens. Through combinations of images and resonant language free of abstraction come the momentary accomplishment of our best selves, moments of transcendence when we as readers can say, "Ah, that's the way it is," or "I wish I had said that," or "I've never looked at things in quite this way." The most successful poets (who can begin to name them all?) live in these worlds of poetry and prose simultaneously. They poach on one world to feed the other. No matter how ethereal their musings, no matter how errant their literary ramblings, they keep, as Thoreau enjoins us, one hand on the huckleberry bush. The material world provides occasion for a leap into the other world, an immersion in transcendence for as long as the poem we've just read sustains itself in our consciousness. For as long as we give it our fickle attention.

Canadian artist Wesley Bates in one of his wood engravings humorously captures this sense of the poet inhabiting the worlds of mind and matter. His "Commedia dell' Arte" depicts a pretentious figure wearing striped leggings and an oversized fur cloak, signifying the artist's contempt for convention, or perhaps his poverty. Assuming a proud pose, he holds before him a page from a manuscript, a feather behind his ear, a shapeless and outlandish hat adorning his head. His profiled cranium is part of a cloud formation; one foot is perched on the neck of a subdued ground hog, wryly signifying the poet's connectedness to the world of the spirit and the world of nature. One look at this parody of literary self-importance should chasten any writer who takes himself or herself too seriously.

The position of poet laureate, with its origins in the 17th century, began as a life appointment in the royal household of

English kings with the expectation that the person selected should compose poems for national occasions or ceremonies at court whenever called on by the sovereign. Starting in 1668 with John Dryden, those appointed included such notables as William Wordsworth, Alfred, Lord Tennyson, and Ted Hughes, the husband of American poet Sylvia Plath, as well as others whose names are all but forgotten. In 1985 the tradition was adopted in this country, the holder also serving as consultant in poetry to the Library of Congress. The first recipient was Robert Penn Warren (1905-1989), a native of Guthrie, Kentucky, and those who have followed represent the full range and diversity of our nation's literary artists. In the early Nineties the Kentucky General Assembly passed a bill providing for the selection of a poet laureate, an honorary two-year position with no specified duties other than to help arrange and celebrate Kentucky Writers Day (April 24, Robert Penn Warren's birthday).

Over the first decade under this refreshingly enlightened legislation, the poet laureate has evolved informally into a position in which the recipient tacitly agrees to promote the literary arts and celebrate Kentucky's rich literary heritage. Increasingly, there is an expectation that the recipient willingly crisscross the state giving readings, doing workshops, speaking at civic clubs, visiting universities and public schools at every level. Part of the mission is to raise the level of awareness among Kentuckians about creative writing and life of the mind. Part is to recognize Kentucky's rich literary tradition while promoting writing among the young and old alike to fuel that tradition. Such stumping has paid off. As James Baker Hall and others have pointed out, three of the last eight Yale Younger Poets have been Kentuckians. In classrooms over the state there is a renewed commitment to nurturing the literary arts. Kentucky is increasingly recognized as a state that has produced important national voices in fiction, drama, and poetry disproportionate to its population, a state that values its rich literary heritage, a state in which the worlds of prose and poetry cohabit in a fruitful marriage.

3

PART I

Origin of the
Poet Laureate

THE POET LAUREATE TRADITION

The term "poet laureate" originated in the myth of Apollo, patron of poets, who tried to seize Daphne, whereupon she turned into a laurel tree. Apollo ordained that the laurels should be the prizes for poets and victors. It is likely that the tradition of the court poet and professional entertainer is the forbearer of the modern poet laureate.[1] Today "Poet Laureate" is the title given to an outstanding or official poet of a state or nation.

Modern usage of the term "poet laureate" began in Great Britain in the 1600's. It was the custom of the English crown to designate a poet to compose odes and other verses in honor of grand state occasions. Poets Geoffrey Chaucer and Edmund Spenser received a royal pension. The stipend of the office was 100 francs a year, with a tierce of canary.

James I created the office of court poet for Ben Jonson in 1617. Sir William Davenant succeeded Jonson in 1638 and held the office until his death in 1668. John Dryden was the first to receive the official title of Poet Laureate; he held it from 1670 to 1688.

Dryden's successors have been Thomas Shadwell (1688-92); Nahum Tate (1692-1715); Nicholas Rowe (1715-18); Laurence Eusden (1718-30); Colley Cibber (1730-57); William Whitehead (1757-85); Thomas Warton (1785-90); Henry James Pye (1790-1813); Robert Southey (1813-43); William Wordsworth (1843-50); Alfred, Lord Tennyson (1850-92); Alfred Austin (1896-1913); Robert Bridges (1913-30); John Masefield (1930-67); C. Day-Lewis (1968-72); Sir John Betjeman (1972-84); and Ted Hughes (1984-). Of these only three can be accounted major poets. Namely: Dryden, Wordsworth, and Tennyson.[2]

POETS LAUREATE OF THE UNITED STATES

Since 1937 the United States has had a "Consultant in Poetry to the Library of Congress." This title was officially changed to "Poet Laureate Consultant in Poetry to the Library of Congress" starting in 1986 by an Act of Congress. Appointment is for a one-year term, but is renewable. Those appointed to these posts are:

Consultants in Poetry to the Library of Congress
- Joseph Auslander, 1937-1941 (Auslander's appointment to the Poetry chair had no fixed term)
- Allen Tate, 1943-1944 (Born in Winchester, Kentucky)
- Robert Penn Warren, 1944-1945 (Born in Guthrie, Kentucky)
- Louise Bogan, 1945-1946
- Karl Shapiro, 1946-1947
- Robert Lowell, 1947-1948
- Leonie Adams, 1948-1949
- Elizabeth Bishop, 1949-1950
- Conrad Aiken, 1950-1952 (First to serve two terms)
- William Carlos Williams (Appointed in 1952 but did not serve)
- Randall Jarrell, 1956-1958
- Robert Frost, 1958-1959
- Richard Eberhart, 1959-1961
- Louis Untermeyer, 1961-1963
- Howard Nemerov, 1963-1964
- Reed Whittemore, 1964-1965
- Stephen Spender, 1965-1966
- James Dickey, 1966-1968
- William Jay Smith, 1968-1970
- William Stafford, 1970-1971
- Josephine Jacobsen, 1971-1973
- Daniel Hoffman, 1973-1974
- Stanley Kunitz, 1974-1976
- Robert Hayden, 1976-1978

- William Meredith, 1978-1980
- Maxine Kumin,1981-1982
- Anthony Hecht, 1982-1984
- Robert Fitzgerald, 1984-1985 (Appointed and served in a health-limited capacity, but did not come to the Library of Congress)
- Reed Whittemore, 1984-1985 (Interim Consultant in Poetry)
- Gwendolyn Brooks, 1985-1986

Poet Laureate Consultants in Poetry to the Library of Congress
- Robert Penn Warren, 1986-1987
- Richard Wilbur, 1987-1988
- Howard Nemerov, 1988-1990
- Mark Strand, 1990-1991
- Joseph Brodsky, 1991-1992
- Mona Van Duyn, 1992-1993
- Rita Dove, 1993-1995
- Robert Hass, 1995-1997
- Robert Pinsky, 1997-2000 (First to serve three consecutive terms. Special Consultants in 1999-2000: Rita Dove, Louise Glück, and W.S. Merwin)
- Stanley Kunitz, 2001-2002
- Billy Collins 2002-2003)
- Louise Glück 2003-

Robert Penn Warren, first to be designated U.S. Poet Laureate, and one of America's most distinguished scholars and writers, was born in Guthrie, Kentucky, on April 24, 1905. He is the only person to have been awarded the Pulitzer Prize in both fiction and poetry, and, having won twice in poetry, is the only three-time Pulitzer winner.

THE KENTUCKY POETS LAUREATE

The Kentucky poet laureate position was established in 1926 by an act of the General Assembly. Prior to 1991, poets were appointed by the General Assembly to lifetime terms, and several poets often held the position simultaneously. In 1991, new legislation provided for appointment by the governor to a two-year term.

1926	J.T. Cotton Noe	Acts Ch.368. P.1042,HJR 16
1928	Edward G. Hill	Gov. Appointment
1945	Mrs. Louise Phillips	Gov. Appointment
1954	Edwin Carlisle Litsey	SJR 10
1954	Jesse Hilton Stuart	SJR 10
1956	Lowell Allen Williams	HJR 5
1974	Lillie D. Chaffin	HJR 42
1976	Senator Tom Mobley	SR 66
1978	Agnes O'Rear	HJR 5
1984	Soc Clay	HR 107 and 168
1984	Lee Pennington	HR 152
1984	Paul Salyers	HJR 95
1986	Dale Faughn	HR 49
1986	Jim Wayne Miller	HR 128
1986	Henry E. Pilkenton	HR 88
1990	James H. Patton, Jr.	HR 47
1995-97	James Still	Gov. Appointment
1997-99	Joy Bale Boone	Gov. Appointment
1999-01	Richard Taylor	Gov. Appointment
2001-03	James Baker Hall	Gov. Appointment
2003-	Joe Survant	Gov. Appointment

THE 1991 KENTUCKY POET LAUREATE STATUTE

The Kentucky Poet Laureate Program was established to honor outstanding Kentucky writers and promote participation in the literary arts of the state.

The process for selection of Kentucky Poet Laureate was newly established (or redefined) in 1991 by the Kentucky General Assembly. According to the provisions of KRS 153.600, the Poet Laureate is appointed by the governor for a two-year term with accompanying duties. The word "poet" in the position's title is interpreted in its broadest sense to include persons whose accomplishments are in any of the recognized literary forms (e.g., poetry, fiction, biography, playwriting, etc.). Currently, nominees for the position are selected by the Kentucky Arts Council and forwarded to the Governor.

Qualifications for the position include the following: (1) Publication of a written body of work which is informed by living in Kentucky; (2) critical acclaim for the work's high degree of creativity and clarity of form and style as demonstrated by the receipt of special honors, awards, and other forms of recognition; (3) capacity to promote the literary arts in Kentucky through readings and/or public presentations.

Minimum duties of the Kentucky Poet Laureate over the two years of office are to make a presentation at the annual Kentucky Writers' Day and to promote the literary arts in Kentucky through readings of his or her work at meetings, seminars, and conferences across the state.

The Kentucky Poet Laureate holds the position from January 1 to December 31 and serves without salary but receives a $5,000 honorarium to cover travel expenses during the two-year term.

Poet Laureate nominations may be made by individuals or organizations within or outside of Kentucky. Nominees must be a resident of Kentucky with a long association with the commonwealth, as well as a writer of any of the recognized literary forms.

PART II

Kentucky Poets Laureate

JAMES THOMAS COTTON NOE
(b. 1864 – d. 1953)
Poet Laureate 1926

Cotton Noe was Kentucky's first officially chosen poet laureate, named by the Kentucky General Assembly in March, 1926.

Noe, poet and educator, was born in Washington County, Kentucky, near Springfield, on May 2, 1864. He was educated in Springfield and Perryville, Kentucky public schools. He then attended Cornell University, the University of Chicago, and Franklin College in Indiana.

He married Sidney Stanfill; they had two sons and one daughter. Noe died in California on November 9, 1953, and his remains were returned to the Lexington Cemetery, in the state that he loved.

As an adult, Noe officially adopted the name "Cotton" after having been nicknamed in his youth because of his light-colored hair.

Noe practiced law in Springfield, Kentucky for four years and then turned to teaching. After receiving his doctorate from Franklin College he taught and was principal of high schools in Kentucky and Indiana for four years. He later served on the faculties of Cumberland College in Williamsburg, Kentucky, and Lincoln Memorial University in Harrogate, Tennessee. In 1908, Noe joined the faculty at the University of Kentucky where he remained until his retirement in 1934.[3]

Noe described himself in the preface of his book *Tip Sams*, as a teacher, not a professional poet. "There are more poets in the state more worthy of the honor and more able to serve Kentucky in the laureate capacity, if any service were demanded," he wrote.

Noe's books of poetry, which are out of print and have become rare, include *The Loom of Life* (1912); *The Blood of Rachel* (1916); *Tip Sams of Kentucky and Other Poems* (1926); *The Valley of Parnassus* (1953); *Oollooloon. In Kentucky, A Brief Anthology of Kentucky Poetry*, and *Tip Sams Again* (1947).

His most noted poetry, *Tip Sams of Kentucky and Other Poems and Dramas*, is still sought by collectors of regional poetry, simply because it contains the first print of "Tip Sams," the celebrated poem of plain life back in the hills of old Kentucky.[4]

TIP SAMS

— from *Tip Sams Again*

Tip Sams had twins
And a razor-back sow,
Five dogs and a mule
And an old roan cow;
A bone-spavined filly
And a one-room house
And a little wrinkled woman
Just as meek as a mouse.
Old Tip raised tobacco
And he trafficked in skins.
For he had seven sons
In addition to the twins,
And every mother's son,
And the little mammy, Jude,
Smoke a pipe all day
And the twins both chewed.
But Tip kept a-digging
And he never lost heart,
For the dogs hunted rabbits
And they caught a right smart;
And the bone-spavined filly
And the mule pulled a plow,
And the acorn-fattened farrow
Of the razor-back sow.
But here the story closes
Of my little romance,
For the seven sons are sleeping
On the battlefields of France;
But their daddy grows tobacco
And trafficks still in skins,
And the little wrinkled mammy
Has another pair of twins.

Noe's purpose, as well as his understanding of the common man, his humor, his warmth, his insight, unfolds as you read his words and feel the affection that he has for nature's finest gift, its people. Perhaps these lines from "Poets In Heaven" demonstrate what Noe wished to achieve by his poetry.[5]

POETS IN HEAVEN
        — from *Tip Sams Again*

I do not crave a poet's name
Nor have I longed for fame;
But when I'm gone if I can know
My verse has made some heart to glow
With love with worthy folk
Who daily toil, yet wear the yoke
Of poverty, I am sure that I
Shall be content beyond the sky.

EDWARD GAY HILL
(b. 1883 – d. 1937)
Poet Laureate, 1928

Edward Gay Hill was born in Ocean Springs, Mississippi on August 17, 1883, a son of Felix Robertson and Ordalis Mayes Hill. His father was a Methodist minister in Louisville. In 1905 he married May Effie, a native of Henry County, Kentucky. They had one daughter, Marjorie Hill Robertson.

Hill was designated as Poet Laureate by Governor Flem D. Sampson on October 1, 1928, in appreciation of his poem "Abraham Lincoln The Man." Hill's verses were published in book form and used as a daily feature in the old *Herald Post*.

Hill was commissioned a Lieutenant Commander in the Naval Reserve Air Force. He died on November 8, 1937, while on a routine trip, when his Navy amphibian plane crashed in Jacksonville, Florida. He had been a world traveler, traveling around the world once and six times to Europe.[6]

On the walls of Hill's office were two official documents: one, issued by Gov. Edwin P. Morrow in 1923, proclaiming him a commodore of the Ohio and all Kentucky rivers, and their tributaries; the other, a document signed by Gov. Flem D. Sampson proclaiming him a poet laureate.

Edward Gay Hill received his preparatory education at Smith's Academy, a department of Washington University in St. Louis. He also attended the Louisville Male High School and graduated from the University of Louisville Law School in 1903. Hill began practicing law the same year. He was affiliated with Falls City Lodge, Free and Accepted Masons, and a member of the Fourth Avenue Methodist Episcopal Church, South.

Hill was one of the leading speakers throughout the state during the 1919-1920 gubernatorial races and was attributed with much of the success of the election of Governor Morrow.

He also was a member of the Pendennis Club. He was an editor of *The American Red Man* for several years. "It has been said that Mr. Hill made more speeches in Kentucky on behalf of the government during the war than any other 'Four Minute Man' in the state."[7]

Mr. Hill was the author of two books of poems. *The Home of Aegeus* published in 1920, and *The Shadow Voice* in 1928.

THE SHADOW VOICE

There is a Voice that speaks in solitude
Within the hearts of men who wait, imbued
With honest yearnings for undimmed sight,
For Truth to speak; who seek unprismed light
To guide them to the goal where Truth was born:
A mystic Shadow-Voice whose words are shorn
Of myth, deception and self-binding fear,—
That breathed before the birth of knowledge here!

It was because of the poem, "Abraham Lincoln The Man" that Hill was commissioned poet laureate by Governor D. Sampson.

ABRAHAM LINCOLN THE MAN
— from *The Shadow Voice*

A gain we pay our homage to The Man—
B orn, like the Nazarene, of low estate,
R reared in the school of toil, the hand of Fate
A lotting him to end what man began,
H e walked, as God's own messenger, God's way
A nd, striking yokes from lash-bent backs of men,
M ade serfdom outlaw by his mighty pen!

L ighted by vision of a better day,
I nspired by love of man to do his task,
N o stronger purpose dwelt in any breast.
C ontrite and clean of heart he wore no mask.
O nly that he, each day, might do his best
L ived he his life till it became sublime—
N o nobler man was ever born of Time!

LOUISE SCOTT PHILLIPS
(b. 1911 - d. 1983)
Kentucky's Sesquicentennial Poet Laureate, 1945

Louise Scott Phillips was born in Kuttawa, Kentucky on August 5, 1911 to Arch and Jennie Scott. She graduated from Lyon County High School in 1929 and later ran a dress shop in Kuttawa.

Louise Scott's first marriage was to Eugene Phillips. In 1958 she married Benny Sandow. She died in 1983 and was buried in Kuttawa's Doom's Cemetery.

Kentucky governor Keen Johnson named her "Poet Laureate of the Sesquicentennial" in 1945. Phillips, from Paducah at that time, was selected after winning a statewide poetry contest sponsored by the Sesquicentennial Commission with cooperation of the Kentucky Federation of Women's Clubs.

Her books include *Day and Nights at Knights* and *Deep End* published by Hunter H. Martin, Paducah, 1945. Many of her poems were published in the local newspapers.[8]

MEMORIES FROM CHILDHOOD
— from *Deep End*

In the evening when the twilight
       Gathers round my cottage door,
I sit alone in the deepening shadows
       And dream about the days of yore.
Again I see an humble cottage
       Perched upon a lonely hill;
I smell the fragrance of the lilacs,
       I hear the robin's chanting trill.

Dimly to my recollection
       Comes the field of waving grain;
Once more I see the young tobacco
       Spreading wide its leaves of green.
I dream about the white sheep grazing,
       On the green hills far away;

I seem to feel the crunch of brown earth
       'Neath my feet as oft I'd stray
O'er the fresh-plowed, upturned sod,
       To meet my Dad at close of day.
The wind blew duskily about me,
       On those long-past summer eves,
As I watched the fireflies glimmer
       Above the wheat field's dimming sheaves.

I recall the one-room schoolhouse,
       And the trail up to its door,
Where the teacher patiently

23

Tried to fill young head with lore.
Again I see the village church,
        And the winding path I trod;
Remember clear a voice expounding
        The truth of an Almighty God.

In my memories I linger
        Near the mound of greening earth,
Where my father long has rested
        By the one who gave me birth.
'Tis so sweet in early evening,
        In the sun's last golden glow,
To recall the scenes of childhood,
        And the days of long ago!

EDWIN CARLISLE LITSEY
(b.1874 – d. 1970)
Poet Laureate, 1954

Edwin Litsey was born at Beechland, Kentucky, June 3, 1874. He was the son of William Henry and Sarah Elizabeth (Johnston) Litsey. He married Carrie Rachel Selceman on June 5, 1900 in Springfield, Kentucky. She died in 1910 and he never remarried. They had one daughter, Sarah Selceman Litsey, also a writer and poet. Litsey died February 3, 1970 at the age of 95, and was buried in the Ryder Cemetery in Lebanon, Kentucky.

Litsey was educated in the local public and private schools but did not attend college. At the age of seventeen he entered the banking business by emptying waste baskets at the Marion National Bank in Lebanon, where he was a lifelong employee, continuing to work at the bank into his nineties.[9]

Litsey was the author of ten novels and two poetry books. At the age of twenty-four his first book was published, a fantasy novel, *The Princess of Gramfalon* (1898). His second book *The Love Story of Abner Stone* was published in 1902. In 1904, he won first prize in *The Black Cat*, story contest, with "In the Court of God," beating out more than ten thousand competitors.

He found his subjects and settings in his native south-central Kentucky, particularly in the counties of Marion, Washington, and Nelson. In 1905, he published *The Race of the Swift*, a series of seven animal stories similar in style to those of Jack London. In *The Man from Jericho*, in 1911, he made use of local subjects such as horse racing, hunting, and chicken fighting. *Grist* was written in 1927. Perhaps Litsey's most successful novel, *Stones for Bread*, 1940, is a story about two lonely brothers.

Litsey's volumes of poetry include *Spindrift* (1915), *Shadow Shapes* (1929), and *The Filled Cup* (1935). His realistic poetry and fiction remain as powerful and accurate records of rural Kentucky life.

His poem, "What of Tomorrow" won first prize in a nationwide contest sponsored by the Poetry Society in Virginia, 1964. He was often published in the Louisville *Courier-Journal* and the local newspapers. Litsey's biography is in *Who's Who in America* and *Who's Who in Kentucky*. Also, he was featured in *Principal Poets of the World* (an English publication).

In 1954, Litsey and Jesse Stuart were appointed joint poet laureates of Kentucky. Litsey was called the poet laureate of central Kentucky and Stuart the poet laureate of eastern Kentucky.

Litsey was one of Marion County's most distinguished citizens. He was said to find the drama of banking in the depositor, not the deposit. In serving two generations of Marion countians, he never failed to look through the barred window and see the human beings on the other side. And he never failed to relish quitting time, as he wrote: [10]

> " . . . Not far away I know that there is a peace,
> A brook, a bird, a tree, a blooming flower
> A spot where my jailed soul can find release,

And gain true riches from each passing hour.
My mind's eye often sees, through bar and grille,
The sunlight lying on a quiet hill."

"Much of his poetry, like these lines from 'Song For Spring,'
reads like a pale echo of Wordsworth or Shelley," wrote Wade
Hall.[11]

SONG OF SPRING

Now is the time the leaves rejoice,
In the ardent sun's embrace,
And the whispering wind becomes a voice

Above the earth's glad face.
Glowing with beauty is the sod,
Bursting with bloom the trees;
Thrilling with life each bud and pod
To the soft kiss of the breeze.
Pixy and sprite hold gay carousel
In the dell where a brooklet flows
White elf and fay hold open house
At the sign of the Lily and Rose.

JESSE HILTON STUART
(b. 1907 – d. 1984)
Poet Laureate, 1954

Jesse Stuart,[12] author, poet and teacher, was born on August 8, 1907 to tenant farmers Mitchell and Martha Hilton Stuart, in northeastern Kentucky's Greenup County,

Stuart married Naomi Deane Norris on October 14, 1939; they had one daughter, Jessica Jane. He died February 17, 1984, and was buried in Plum Grove Cemetery in Greenup County.

Stuart graduated from Greenup High School in 1926 and from Lincoln Memorial University in Harrogate, Tennessee in 1929. He then returned to Greenup County Schools to teach. Stuart began writing about the hill people of his section of Kentucky while still a college student. He eventually became one of America's best-known and best-loved writers.[13]

Stuart served as a teacher in Greenup County's one-room schools and as high school principal and county school superintendent. These experiences served as the basis for his auto-biographical book, *The Thread That Runs So True* in 1949. The president of the National Education Association called this book "the best book on education written in the last fifty years." The book dramatized the need for educational reform in Kentucky.[14]

Collections of his poems include: his first collection published in *Harvest of Youth* (1930*); Songs of a Mountain Plowman,* written between 1929 and 1931*; Man With a Bull-Tongued Plow* (1934); *Hold April* (1962); *Autumn Love Song* and *Kentucky Is My Land.*

His autobiography, *Beyond Dark Hills*, was published in 1938 and his first novel, *Trees of Heaven* in 1940. His first short story collection was *Head O' W-Hollow* (1936), followed by *Men of the Mountains* (1941) and *Tales of the Plum Grove Hills*, (1946). Stuart published more than a dozen novels and autobiographical works. *Taps for Private Tussie* (1943) is an award-winning satirical look at New Deal relief and its effect on the hill people's self-reliance, and *God's Oddling* (1960) is a biography of Stuart's father.[15]

Stuart also wrote a number of highly regarded books for children and youth. Prominent among them are *The Beatinest Boy* (1953) and *A Penny's Worth of Character* (1954). Others *are Old Ben, A Ride with Huey the Engineer,* and *The Rightful Owner* (1960). *Huey, the Engineer*, a small novel (1960), was a collector's item, with publication limited to six hundred copies.[16]

He has two hundred articles and approximately two thousand poems published in magazines and in his collection of poems. The number of published books is 60 and there are 460 short stories.

His awards and honors include: 1934, Jeanette Sewal Davis Poetry Prize, 1937; Guggenheim Fellowship Award for Creative Writing and European Travel, 1941; Academy of Arts and Sciences Award, 1943; Thomas Jefferson Memorial Award, 1944;

29

Honorary Doctor of Literature from the University of Kentucky, 1946; *Man with a Bull-Tongued Plow* was selected as one of the 100 Best Books in America and one of the 1000 Great Books of the World, 1949; *The Thread That Runs So True* was selected as the best book in 1949 by the National Education Association.[17]

In 1952, *Taps for Private Tussie* was selected as one of the Masterpieces of World Literature and in 1961 he received $5,000 from The Academy of American Poets Awards for "Distinguished Service to American Poetry." [18]

Stuart suffered a major heart attack in 1954. During his convalescence, he wrote daily journals that became *The Year of My Rebirth.*

LEAVES FROM A PLUM GROVE OAK

—from *Man With a Bull-Tongue Plow* [19]

Sir:
I am a farmer singing at the plow
And as I take my time to plow along
A steep Kentucky hill, I sing my song—
A one-horse farmer singing at the plow!
I do not sing the songs you love to hear;
My basket songs are woven from the words
Of corn and crickets, trees and men and birds.
I sing the strains I know and love to sing.
And I can sing my lays like singing corn,
And flute them like a fluting gray corn-bird;
And I can pipe them like a hunter's horn
All of my life these are the songs I've heard.
And these crude strains no critic can call art,
Yours very respectfully, Jesse Stuart.

MAN WITH A BULL-TONGUED PLOW
— from *Kentucky Is My Land* [20]

I didn't have any choice
as to where I was born,
But if I had had my choice,
I would have chosen Kentucky.
And if could have chosen
wind to breathe, I would
have chosen a Kentucky wind
with the scent of cedar,
pinetree needles,
green tobacco leaves, pawpaw,
persimmon and sassafras.
I would have chosen too,
Wind from the sawbriar and
greenbriar blossoms.

"Kentucky is neither southern, northern, eastern, western, It is the
core of America. If these United States can be called a body
Kentucky is its heart."   — Jesse Stuart

LOWELL ALLEN "AL" WILLIAMS
(b. 1907 – d. 1995)
Poet Laureate 1956

Lowell Allen Williams was born January 3, 1907 in Macon County, Missouri. He graduated from high school in 1926 in LaPlata, Missouri, then went to study at Missouri Valley College.

He married Gladys Lovelace from Cunningham, Kentucky in 1935. They had two children, Patricia and Ben Allen. Once rooted in Kentucky he worked as a mechanical inspector for the Union Carbide Nuclear Company.

Poet, speaker, and civic leader, Lowell Allen Williams wrote of the everyday happenings of ordinary people for thirty years. Williams' work is summed up by the popular Kentucky writer, Fred Newman, in these words: "People who like the kind of poetry that gets next to the heart will revel in Williams' poems calculated to fit every mood, shot through with human feeling."

Of his thousands of poems, about one hundred have been published privately in several booklets. He also was a public speaker and wrote skits for radio and television. His books include: *This Life We Live, Home Is My Kentucky*, and *Across the Wide, Green Valley*.

He ran a poetry column, "Poems to Live By," regularly in the *Carlisle County News*, and from time to time in the *Mayfield Messenger*, the *Cairo Evening Citizen*, and the *Ballard Yeoman*.[21]

An appropriate resolution was introduced to make Williams the poet laureate, but the 1954 session had proclaimed "the" poet laureate to be Jesse Stuart, W-Hollow, and Edwin Carlisle Litsey, Lebanon. So the resolution was changed to make him "a" poet laureate in 1956.

Across the Wide, Green Valley is expressive of the heritage, hope and character of America and the people of the earth. Mr. Williams' verses have been used on the air, in pulpits, and classrooms in a dozen states and abroad. This volume was reprinted five times. Many schools in Kentucky selected the book as preferred reading text.[22]

A PRAYER

Lord, teach me diligence, to see the part that Thou hast
    laid for me,
Seal my lips against the word that I may speak, if being
    heard It may bring sorrow or despair, to brothers who
    are laboring there.
That I may do my job, how small, that at Thy final
    beckoning call
My skein is woven strong and tight, and my small thread,
    in pattern bright
The finished cloth in colors gay, will make a better,
    shining day,
Thus let my feeble thread shine through in any job that I
    may do.

OBSERVIN'
    — from *Across the Wide, Green Valley*

That picture's hung there
        Ten years now or more,
With its cord and its fringe
        By the side of the door.

And it's just struck my fancy
        As being quite nice
Of the taste of the buyer—
        The scene and the price.

Now the frame isn't much,
        A dull sort of gray,
But the boughs on the willow
        In the breeze seem to sway.

The creek is as smooth
        As the one by the mill,
And the pink-tinted clouds
        Climbin' back o'er the hill.

Have a feelin' of quiet,
        That gives my soul ease;
Says: "Come rest a while,
        Read a book if you please."

In my fancy and dreams
        I have seen such a place,
Made for fishin' and picnics,
        And swimmin' hole race.

I chide my neglect—
        Am I missing much more?
To think I had ne'er
        Seen that picture before.

LILLIAN D. CHAFFIN
(b. 1925 – d. 1993)
Associate Poet Laureate, 1974

Lillian "Lillie" Chaffin[23] was born to Kenis and Fairybelle Dorton at Varney, Kentucky, in Pike County, February 1, 1925. She married Thomas Chaffin in 1942 and was the mother of one son, Thomas Randall. Chaffin married Vernon Kash in 1983 after the death of her first husband.

In *A World of Books* Chaffin describes her desire to write at an early age. As a child, she would retreat to the roof of her home, there to daydream and write. Although Chaffin quit Johns Creek High School at the age of seventeen, she later returned and graduated valedictorian in 1947.[24] She attended Akron University from 1951 through 1952 and earned her bachelors degree from

Pikeville College in 1958 and a masters from Eastern Kentucky University in 1971.

Chaffin worked twenty-eight years as an elementary school teacher and librarian at Bevins School, Kemper School, and Johns Creek High School. She taught and lectured in writing workshops at Berea College, Eastern Kentucky University, Pikeville College, and the University of Kentucky.

Chaffin also worked as a freelance writer and her first book, *A Garden is Good* in 1963. Among her other works are *Bear Weather* (1968) (named best book by *The New York Times*); *I Have a Tree* (1969) (named best book by American Pen Women); *Freeman* (1972); *Eighth Day Thirteenth Moon* (1974) (nominated for the Pulitzer Prize); and *A Stone for Sisyphus* (1967) (winner of the International Prize for Poetry). Also, *John Henry McCoy* (1971) and *Appalachian History and Other Poems* (1980).

Chaffin was recognized by *Epoch*, Cornell University's literary magazine as one of the America's top poets. She was named Teacher of the Year and Distinguished Alumnus of Eastern Kentucky University and Pikeville College, as well as being awarded an Honorary Doctorate of Letters degree from both.

In 1995, Chaffin endowed the Lillie Chaffin-Kash literary award. The fund provides an annual award to "celebrate Appalachian Writings."[25]

OBSERVATION
— From *A Stone for Sisyphus* [26]

Rain drops, sink slowly
and deeper now that earth
is undraped.

Leaves and grass diminished,
land is quiet, receptive
as child at first bath.

Untangled from summer,
all is even-smooth
and waiting.

NO PRAISE FOR ONCE
— From A Stone for Sisyphus [27]

This day I bring no awards, no trophies.
Air moves in and out me with
the same design and the same ease
as blood flows, mechanically. Death
    has all dominion, and is no ambition
    for ending evil, is no invention
    for gaining new worlds.

There are no crowds at funerals. We
stand separate, each in the wrath
of a private loss or humble piety
of subdued wills, quiet, giving no breath
    to rages against decay,
    against the shaky hold we may or may
    not keep against madness.

It is not time yet, if it ever is, to tease
from our drained thoughts and set at hearth
a praise for once, not with this emptiness;
to do so would be a truce, false shibboleth.
    I do not mean
    to do so, though I never win.
    Only this battle is reality.

SENATOR TOM MOBLEY
(b. 1916 – d. 1996)
Poet Laureate, 1976

Tom Mobley was born in Elizabethtown, Kentucky on June 16, 1916, the youngest of three children. He graduated from Elizabethtown High School and from Bowling Green University in 1938. He married Ona Retta Lemming of Louisville in 1939. they had two children, Randy and John. He later married Anna Lee Johnson of Virgie, Pike County, Kentucky. This marriage produced a daughter, Mary Chase Mobley in 1958.[28]

Mobley died October 19, 1996 in Inverness, Florida and was returned to Bowling Green's Fairview Cemetery.

The Hardin County native was vice president of Kosmos-Portland Cement Company in Louisville and a distributor for Shell and Ashland Oil. He began his legislative career in 1952, when he was elected to the state House of Representatives from Warren County. He served as highway commissioner in Bowling Green in 1956 and served in the Kentucky Senate from 1972-1980. He was a World War II Navy veteran, and a member of the boards of directors of Brookhaven Children's Home and the Methodist Evangelical Hospital.[29]

Tom Mobley was nominated for poet laureate by Senator William Gentry from Bardstown, Nelson County, Kentucky. From the resolution designating Senator Mobley as Poet Laureate:

> WHEREAS, Tom Mobley, a valued Senator, has advanced the wealth of Kentucky poetry with his famous Senate "Poem for Posterity," and
> WHEREAS, Senator Tom Mobley is equally gifted with cement or lament; and WHEREAS, through his works, has created for future citizens a legacy of what it means to be a proud Kentuckian and poetic Senator. Section 1. That Senator Tom Mobley, District 19, Seat 21, be designated as Senator Poet in Residence and as a Poet Laureate for the Commonwealth of Kentucky.[30]

According to members of Mobley's family, his poetry was written "for fun" and as political commentary, rather than with the goal of attaining literary excellence. His son says that Senator Gentry who nominated him for poet laureate "would have been more likely to have heard my father's reciting of a limerick" rather than an attempt at serious poetry.[31] Mobley used poetry to good advantage in pointing out what he perceived as the shortcomings of his political opponents in the following poem cited by Gentry:

POEM FOR POSTERITY

Members of the Senate will vote today
Whether or not to increase their pay
Senators are surely not so dumb
To refuse more money their heads would be numb
Rep. Albert Robinson saw the light
Many years of voting NO was not right.

Had voted no five times and quaked in his shoes
For fear the other representatives votes no would choose
To keep them all from getting more money
To live in this land of milk and honey
I've seen many pay bills sessions come and go

They always pass if promoted just so.
I've seen many members stand up and say
I knew when I came here what this job would pay
These are the ones who then vote NO
Then hope the Aye votes are counted just so
That they'll get their checks same as the rest
Telling their constituents they did their best
To keep the pay raises from being passed
Said they didn't want more money and in the same gasp
Swallowed hard on what was said knowing full well
That the story they told would not send them to hell

There comes a time in every Senator's career
To show his backbone and the time is this year.
Stand up on your feet for all to know
So every one here can see you show
Your colors you truly want to bare
Your new pay check you deserve to share.
Take it . . . Enjoy it . . . Share with your wife
Spend it on your family . . . rightfully enjoy your life.

AGNES TODD SAFFELL O'REAR
(b. 1896 – d. 1990)
Poet Laureate, 1978

Agnes O'Rear [32] was designated poet laureate by the General Assembly on March 7, 1978.

O'Rear, wife, mother, homemaker, talented seamstress, author, songwriter, artist, and poet, was born March 1, 1895 in the home of her grandparents, James and Mattie Berry Saffell, in Frankfort, Kentucky. Her father, Phythian Saffell, was a musician and a grandson of Benjamin Berry of Woodford County. Her mother, Frances Allen Taylor Saffell, was the youngest daughter of Col. E.H. Taylor, Jr., famous distiller and political leader; his wife was Frances Miller Johnson Taylor.

O'Rear was a graduate of the Kentucky Female Orphan School (now Midway College) in Midway, Kentucky. She married James B. O'Rear in 1914, and they had five children, two of whom died in infancy. Mrs. O'Rear died in 1990 and is buried in the Frankfort Cemetery. She is survived by three daughters: Pat Perry, Nancy Dunstall, and Jinks Barnard.

Mrs. O'Rear, began writing poetry in her early twenties to entertain her children. She never considered her "jingles" poetry until her husband died in 1975; then she started taking her writing seriously.[33]

O'Rear described her writing as strictly spontaneous. On some nights she wrote as many as many as five poems in a sitting.[34]

Three of her books are found in the Kentuckian collection of the Kentucky state library: *From Where I Sit: A Book of Poems*, *A Poem to Kentucky*, and *With Love: A Book of Poems*. She later published another book with the help of her daughter, Jinks O'Rear Barnard, *It Came To Me*.

O'Rear describes her life in the following poem (with her daughter's annotations in parenthesis.[35]):

AUTOBIOGRAPHY

Been thinking it over
decided to write
my autobiography, keeping it light

don't mean to be bragging,
just want to relate
the first-hand experience
dealt me by fate

I've climbed up a mountain (Rockies, the Grand Canyon,
        Yellowstone)
I've lived on a plain (Skiff, in Alberta, Canada)
I've flown to far places, and then back again

42

I've driven a Lincoln
A Model T (lost in a blizzard in Canada)
I've ridden a horse (oh, woe is me) (in Kentucky and
        Canada)
I've written a book (for children)
It's not very long
I've painted a picture (of Hereford cattle)
I've written songs (one is "When the Bluegrass is Blue in
        Kentucky")
I've tailored a suit (rawhide, with badger claw buttons)
I've learned to bake bread (salt-rising)
Have won, with my flowers, blue ribbons and red.

I've hunted for ducks (Alberta, Canada)
I've fished in the sea (Naples, Florida)
I've square-danced and waltzed (Canada and Frankfort)
Hit a ball off a tee (Naples, Florida)
I've plowed with a tractor
I've milked a cow (Glenary Farm, Franklin County, KY)

I've learned to keep books (Woodford Hereford Farm,
        Woodford County)
I'm keeping them now.
The best for the last,
I always save
And I promise to stick to facts, not rave.
I've raised us a family (three daughters)
Got grandchildren too (nine)
I really have lived since that day I won you.

Now, autobiographies
Obviously end
Before the person by whom they are penned.

"So I'll add as a finis
there's lot more to do
that so far, I just haven't got 'round to."

43

CLARENCE "SOC" HENRY CLAY
(b. 1937)
Poet Laureate, 1984

Soc Clay was born September 23, 1935 at Lloyd, Kentucky in Greenup County. He is the son of Thomas Charles and Justine Gullet Clay. Clay attended Biggs Grade School in Lloyd, Kentucky, and graduated from McKell High School. He and his wife Wanda live at Fern Hollow, also in Greenup. They have three children: Kerry Randal, Carla Jo, and Thomas Charles Clay.

Clay's counts the following among his awards: named Poet Laureate by Governor Martha Layne Collins and the 1983 Kentucky General Assembly and recipient of Kentucky Conservation Communicator of 1984 and 1986. He is also recipient of the distinguished Tom Rollins Award and Lifetime Achievement Award presented by the Southeastern Outdoor Press Association. He is an active member, founder, and past president of the

Kentucky Outdoor Press Association, an active member and past president of the Ohio Outdoor Writers Association, and an active member and past director of the Outdoor Writers of America Association.

He is an award-winning, full time, freelance writer and still photographer with credits appearing in most major outdoor publications in North America. Clay is a frequent contributor to *Ohio Sportsman, Fishing Facts, Outdoor Life, Wing & Shot, Gun Dog, Wildfowl, Ducks Unlimited, North American Fisherman, Petersen's, Southern Sportsman's Journal, Kentucky Afield, Bassmaster, On The Road*, and many others. He is a major contributor to over one hundred major outdoors titles and general interest magazines, books and periodicals in the United States and Canada.

Clay says that "Quetico" has been a much published piece.[36]

QUETICO

Eastward bound from Ely Town
We fly on the Otter's gold wings
To the deep blue waters of Lac La Croix
Where the silent wilderness sings.

Now dip your paddles deep me lads
The pale ghost of the northwoods moans
There's miles to make and portages to take
And a time for muscles to groan.

We'll follow the path of the Voyageurs my friends
And cuss 'cross the trail of deep muck
And through this land unspoiled my man
We'll trust in our guide and to luck.

We'll catch the leaping smallies boys
We vow from stem to stern

45

And make a hike for the northern pike
Whose secret lairs we will learn.

The knife will flash through walleye flesh
For fillets fit for the pan
And spuds will fry and coffee boil high
As wild stories are told to the man.

The night doeth come and campfire hums
And stars are a million on high
And somewhere they say in this land far away
The voice of the timberwolf cries.

In six days' time we'll finish the paddle
And return to the habits of men
But a final round of the loon's eerie sound
Reminds us of where we have been.

The northwoods ghosts returns again
On a wind that is autumntime bound
Ye have paddled the Kingdom of God me lads
Now keep in mind what ye've found.

There's places on earth where man makes a stand
And places that's best left alone
And here in the land of the Voyageur's red hand
The bear and the wolf are at home.

So go now in peace and return if you wish
To this world of sweetwater and blue sky
But leave not a trace of Man's might waste
Just footprints to say you passed by.

LEE PENNINGTON
(b. 1939)
Poet Laureate, 1984

Lee Pennington was born May 1, 1939, in White Oak, Kentucky, the son of Andrew Virgil and Mary Ellen Lawson Pennington. He attended Flat Hollow Elementary School and later graduated from McKell High School, Greenup County, Kentucky in 1958. Pennington married Joy Stout, a teacher, on January 28, 1962.[37]

Lee was born ninth of eleven children. He always knew he would go to college, although he didn't know how. Pennington said he eventually used his writing to work and pay his way through school. He credits two great teachers at McKell High School, Jesse Stuart and Mrs. Lena Nevison, for encouraging him to write.

His college education began at the Baldwin-Wallace College in 1958; he then went to San Diego State University in 1961, received a BA from Berea College in 1962, an MA in 1965 from the University of Iowa, and did graduate study at the University of Kentucky in 1966.

Pennington has been a professor of English at Jefferson Community College, Louisville, Kentucky from 1967 to the present. He is also a farmer, editor, news writer, sports editor, publicity writer, columnist, and poet.

He lectures, gives readings, folksong concerts, and story-tellings for universities, festivals, and groups all over America and in foreign countries.

His awards include the Emerson Poetry Award, the Mildred A. Daughtery Award for Contribution to Literature, the Distinguished Contribution to Poetry Award, Magna Cum Laude Award and Honorary Doctorate of Philosophy in Arts.

Pennington's biography is included in: *Who's Who in American Education* (1967), *Kentucky Authors* (1967), *Outstanding Young Men in America* (1969), *Who's Who in Poetry* (1970), *Contemporary Authors* (1978, 1985), *and A Literary History of Kentucky* (1988).

He wrote the script for a 1970 MGM movie *The Moonshine War*. More than a thousand poems have appeared in more than three hundred magazines. His poetry and drama include *Scenes from a Southern Road* (1969), *Wildflower—Poems for Joy* (1970), *Appalachia, My Sorrow* (1976), and *I Knew a Woman* (1977) which has been called "a celebration of women." His work has been compared to the writing of D.H. Lawrence and nominated for a Pulitzer Prize. *The Janus Collection* (1982), is a fusion of his poetry and photography.[38] *April Poems* (1971), was written for Jesse Stuart and his wife, who were in Africa in the spring of 1969. Stuart wrote back, "Of all the things we might miss during this spring, is April in W-Hollow, Kentucky."

POET OF THE FLOWERS [39]

Kentucky woman, against the sun,
I've seen you gather from the hills
Earth flowers and bring them one by one
To grow in places they say no flowers can;
I've seen your gentle hands in love
With growing things—a love which falls
Like rain when April's gone. I've seen
Them bloom as though a magic moon
Touched each tender petal when the dew
Was down. They bloom in sound; they bloom
In song: Poet of the Flowers
Writing for the wind in evening hours.

Pennington published his nineteenth book, *Thigmotropism*, in 1993, and reviews were favorable. Jim Wayne Miller said, "He has discovered a profound metaphor . . . in this beautifully centered book."

THIGMOTROPISM
— from *Thigmotropism* [40]

Behind walls heart vines grow
as if in space exempt of eyes
no blindness is, in great circles
clockwise the search for pole
to hold love's weight upright.

Motion first in the wide open air
strangely slipping around the sun,
the moon, with night always
undone where first touch makes aware
spiral climbing upward to the light.

Even before, as eyes across a dark room,
something pole to vine, vine to pole, is said—
sound without sound, wave without wave,
instead life's weaving on that invisible loom
the waft and warp to hold it tight.

We surely, string and stem, hear
that call, a silent vision sight
when at such greening moment
we concentrically upward take flight.

PAUL SALYERS
(b. 1940)
Poet Laureate, 1984

Paul Salyers was born at Wolf, Kentucky, August 21, 1929. He attended a one-room school at Oakland for eight years, then attended Carter County High School where he graduated in 1947. He received the AB degree from Morehead State University. Salyers lives with his wife Betty on a farm in Olive Hill and they are the parents of six children.

His early life was spent on the farm and at intervals working at Carter Caves State Park. Salyers retired from thirty-two years of teaching in 1989.

Writing always fascinated Salyers; he had his first poem published in the *Olive Hill Times* in 1969. Since then, he has been published in more than one hundred magazines, newspapers, and anthologies. His poems have appeared in the United States, Canada, England, and Scotland.

Salyers has published twenty-six books of poetry. He has been poetry editor for the *Daily Independent*, Ashland, Kentucky, since 1976.

He has served as president of the Kentucky State Poetry Society and held various positions in poetry circles in several states. His name is included in *The International Who's Who in Poetry* and in *Personalities of the South*.

Paul Salyers is a prolific poet. He is known for his sense of humor which he is able to weave into many of his lighter poems without distracting from the real worth. His books have circled the country and he has received many complimentary responses from near and far.[41]

Among Salyer's books are: *Voice of the Hills, The Passing Day, Hounds on the Hill, Thoughts Behind a Plow, Sap With a Sproutin' Hoe, Kentucky Canes, Corkscrews of My Mind, Through My Eyes, Halfway to Heaven, My Native Land*, and many more.

The title poem from the chapbook, *The Road Taken* is an example of how Salyers enjoys taking an idea by another poet in a different direction:[42]

THE ROAD TAKEN

With apologies to Robert, I
took the road that was well traveled
and followed it till it unraveled.
Yet there were times I wondered why.

Sometimes it led me through the brier
and I have scars that do not show.
Pursuing it through rain and snow
sometimes I was short on desire.

Oh there were times I deemed it wise
that I had chosen this fair road
because of gifts on me bestowed.
Oft I was silent in my guise.

But in the middle of life's day
when I had time to meditate,
I wondered if it was too late
to take a look the other way.

Would it be possible to take
a short trek down the other trail
when one is old and used and frail?
A voice cried GO, for pity-sake!

SPRING CHECK
      — from *Lines from a Kentucky Hill*

The dentistry of the hills
is looking good;
Rocks are capped with moss,
deep crevices
are filled with trilliums,
and the trees
are braced
against the wind
to hold the rich black loam.

DALE FAUGHN
(b. 1925)
Poet Laureate, 1986

Dale Faughn was born November 8, 1925 at Lamasco, Lyon County, Kentucky. He attended one and two-room schools through the eighth grade and graduated from Eddyville High School in 1944. Dale is the father of seven children, grandfather of twelve, and great-grandfather of three. He lives on a two hundred, fifty-five acre farm in Freedonia, Kentucky.

Faughn received his BS and his MA from Murray State University "With Distinction." He is certified with a Life Certificate by the Kentucky State Department of Education to teach biology and agriculture. He is in his forty-ninth year of teaching for the Caldwell County school system, and has no plans for retiring.

54

He started writing poetry aboard a transport ship on the way back from the invasion of Iwo Jima. He has published seven books, *Praise and Patriotism, Living the Full Life, Don't Be Ordinary, Showering Our Love, From the Manger to the Mansion, Nurtured by Nature,* and *Observations and Exhortations.*

Faughn has won many awards for his leadership in the community for his services to the schools and the churches. He was awarded the "Citizen of the Year Award" from the Kiwanis, "Poetry Club Founder Award" (1996), and the "Ashland Oil Teacher Achievement Award" (1990). He writes poetry on a great variety of subjects and gives poetry recitals to various groups. His poetry has been published in numerous magazines and newspapers.

Faughn believes that there are those who come into the world and refuse to be ordinary and that life is for the living and there is work to be done. He has devoted his life to the betterment of humankind through service to others, both in his chosen profession and his personal life.[43]

An excerpt from: DARE TO DREAM
— from *Don't Be Ordinary*

When I was back then growing up,
With poverty extreme—
I did not let it get me down—
Instead I chose to dream.

Though times were hard and food was scarce,
I kept my sights ahead;
I knew the time would come for me,
When I could be well fed.

When life seems hard and things look bad,
There still is hope for you—
If you will dream and then work hard
To make your dreams come true.

THE CAN-DO MAN

Success starts in the mind of man,
When he envisions that he can
Reach out and make his dreams come true:
When he is sure what he can do;
Yes, in himself he must believe
Before success he can achieve;
And then when doubts from others rise,
They'll not his boat of dreams capsize;
His course is set; it will not veer;
To him his goals are mighty clear;
I'll tell you now ere you should ask:
This man is equal to the task;
He keeps achieving by his plan—
Because he is a "can-do" man.

Proverbs 23:7
"For as he thinketh in his heart, so is he."

JIM WAYNE MILLER
(b. 1936 – d. 1996)
Poet Laureate, 1986

Jim Wayne Miller was born in Leicester, North Carolina, deep in the Appalachian Mountains, October 21, 1936. He grew up in those mountains, receiving his education from the schools, the people, his parents and grandparents. In 1954, he entered Berea College where he studied English and received his BA.[44]

He continued his studies at Vanderbilt in the Department of Germanic and Slavic Languages and as NDEA Fellow under Donald Davidson and Randall Stewart.

He married Mary Ellen Yates of Carter County, Kentucky in 1958. They have three children: James, Fredrick, and Ruth Ratchliff.[45]

Miller was a professor of German at Western Kentucky University in Bowling Green and served as consultant to Appalachian studies programs in neighboring states. He was considered one of the region's foremost authorities on Appalachian literature[46] and was popular at readings and workshops.

Miller's extensive knowledge of Appalachia is evident in his paper, "Appalachian Culture and History: Part of America's Past and Present and Indicative of its Future" which appeared in *Focus: Teaching English Language Arts* (Winter, 1984), pp 1-12.

He is the author of eight collections of poems and two chapbooks: *Sideswipes* (chapbook, satirical essays), and *The Wisdom of Folk Metaphor* (chapbook, satirical poem). His first collection of poems was *Copperhead Cane* (1964), followed by *The More Things Change, the More They Stay the Same* (1971), *Dialogue With a Dead Man* (1974), *The Mountains Have Come Closer* (1980), *I Have a Place* (1981), *Vein of Words* (1984), *Nostalgia for 70* (1986), *Brier, His Book*, and *Newfound* (1988), which is a lyrical novel of growing up in the Appalachian mountains. A posthumous collection, *The Brier Poems*, was published by Gnomon Press.

Miller was a member of the board of directors of the Jesse Stuart Foundation and one of their editors. He edited Jesse Stuart's *Songs of a Mountain Plowman, Hie to the Hunters, Kentucky is my Land, To Teach, to Love*, and many other books. He also edited an anthology of Appalachian literature and *The Wolfpen Poems*, a collection of James Still's poems.

Awards and honors include: Alice Lloyd Memorial Prize for Appalachian Poetry from Alice Lloyd College in 1967; Sigma Tau Delta Topaz Award for Distinguished Service to the University, Western Kentucky University, 1969; Western Kentucky University faculty award for research and creativity, 1976; Thomas Wolfe Literary Award, for *The Mountains Have Come Closer* in 1980. He received an honorary doctorate of letters from Berea College in 1981. He also received literary awards for poetry, short stories, and translations from the Kentucky Writers Guild, *Green River Review, Appalachian Harvest*, and *Kentucky Poetry Review*.

Several people familiar with *Copperhead Cane* and with his later collections volunteered that they still prefer these poems. Miller said, "And I have never been more pleased with the public reception of a book of my poems than I have been with the reception of these poems. I am somewhat utilitarian in my outlook. I like to ask of anything, even of a poem: 'What is it good for? What's its use?'" [47]

Jim Wayne Miller died an untimely death in 1996. He left a rich heritage, having helped enrich the literary arts in Kentucky by recognizing Kentucky as the "writerly state," and by fostering new writers in the state. He was never too busy to pause to offer advice or assistance to anyone engaged in the pursuit of knowledge.

COPPERHEAD CANE
— from *Copperhead Cane* [48]

Craft carving with fancy on the plain
held in the hand of sleight
knows how to feign
the seasoned stock of need to grave delight.
Often I've seen you make,
by carving a needful sourwood walking stick,
a spiraling snake.
Wrought out of my gnarled grief by that same trick,
these poems are a copperhead cane.

2/17/84

Jesse Stuart, I hope your death today
was mild as this mid-February evening.
And Jesse, I hope your spirit slipped away
so gently no one knew that you were leaving—
and started walking home this afternoon
to W-Hollow, over the rock-ribbled hills.
This is a night for walking, Jess, the moon
hangs in the sky round as a wagon wheel.
I hope your spirit's walking in no hurry
after this death, moving through moonshadows
this mild tonight in mid-February.
I hope you come through old fields, moonlit meadows
home to your Mom and Dad, the place you love,
home to W-Hollow and Plum Grove.

— Jim Wayne Miller

HENRY E. PILKENTON
(b. 1895 – d. 1992)
Poet Laureate, 1986

Henry Pilkenton was born July 20, 1895 in White Mills, Kentucky and died November 2, 1992. At the recommendation of the Kentucky Arts Council, Pilkenton was named Kentucky Poet Laureate in 1986.

Educated in local schools, he graduated from Western Kentucky University. After his service in the army during World War I, he began a career in education.

He taught at Flint Hill School, grades 7-12, then later became founding principal at Lynnvale School in Hardin County. He also coached basketball, taught high school English, history, drama, and other activities.

He married Lela Mae Wortham of White Mills on May 18, 1921 and they had one daughter, Emily Bogard of Elizabethtown, Kentucky.[49]

Pilkenton said it was his aunts who first interested him in poetry as a child by giving him books of nursery rhymes.[50]

Mr. Pilkenton was included in the 1990 edition of *Who's Who in Poetry*. His poems appeared often in the local newspapers and the *Courier-Journal* in Louisville.

His book *Memories, Moods, and Meditations* includes the poems "Pioneer Women," "In the Back Country," "The Christmas Tree at Rockefeller Center," "The Day When I Met You," and White Mills."

THE DAY WHEN I MET YOU

The nights were lonely with dreary days,
No contrast of lights and shadows.
The babbling brook, a dull monotone,
And the birds' songs noisy chatter.
The breeze that whispered in the trees
Was annoying and distressing:
My life was a hopeless labyrinth,
Frustrating and confusing
Until the day when I met you
Who changed it all to music.

Pilkenton often wrote about his younger days when he lived in White Mills. His poem, "White Mills," tells of his memory of the community. "Memories are easy to write about," he said.

WHITE MILLS

The silver stream that runs between
The white cliff and the mill
The wagon bridge, the swimming hole,
The school house on the hill;
The shady streets that run along
The river's peaceful stream,
All rush back in my memory
And form a peaceful dream.

The shady park, the locust trees,
The swings suspended there,
The sheltered nook beneath the cliff,
The cool and fragrant air;
When it's dogwood blossom time
I'll be in Old White Mills.

JAMES H. PATTON, JR.
(b. 1919 – d. 1999)
Poet Laureate, 1990

James "Jim" Patton, Jr. was born in College Grove, Tennessee, June 14, 1919. He attended Ground Academy after high school. There, he met his wife, Jeannie, to whom he was married fifty-six years. They had one son, James H. Patton, III, and three daughters: Donna Fiero, Judy McDonald, and Sara Jenkins.

Patton developed an interest in literature while still a young boy. He was particularly delighted and inspired by the style and language used by the English romantic poets, such as Wordsworth, Keats and Byron [51] and his poetry reflects their influence.

Patton attended Western Kentucky University with plans of a writing career. However, World War II cut his education short, and he was drafted into the United States Army. After the war, he settled in Franklin, Kentucky. There he became a buyer and seller of seed at Franklin Seed and Grain where he worked until he retired in 1984.[52]

Patton's published poems represent a partial compilation of his writing, spanning some fifty years. His general approach and purpose, beyond the sheer pleasure of free expression, was to challenge the reader to think and to act responsibly to make a better world.

After retiring, he continued his writing, completing a second, yet unpublished novel and many new poems. Patton died May 13, 1999 at his home. He was buried in Franklin, Tennessee, in the Mount Hope Cemetery.

Some of Patton's poems have been recognized by the poetry magazine *Alura Quarterly*. His books which he was invited to take to the Kentucky Book Fair are *The Hermit, The Wisdom of the Sphinx and Other Poems*, and *Somewhere in the Scheme*.

MY BROTHER
— From *Somewhere in the Scheme* [53]

Who Lord might my brother be?
And why should someone look to me
To give of what in lawful gain
I lay in store by labor's pain?

Who has the right to beg or ask
The profits of my daily task?
If failure mars another's way
Should I, successful, have to pay?

Oh Lord, I pray to you, define
And draw a clear and narrow line
Of who is brother! Yet I know.
I found him down toward Jericho.

AT SEVEN
— From *Somewhere in the Scheme* [54]

Let me pass on as an autumn leaf on a quiet stream,
Softly, gently, quietly down the way of death.
Let me close my eyes as if asleep in a dream
And thus in solemn slumber take my final breath.

HERITAGE HOPE
— From *The Hermit*

When I shall pass from this short stay
To give the record of the way
I lived, and you someday recall
Our times together, then not at all
Reflect on ugly things you see
But kindly please remember me.

JAMES STILL
(b. 1906 – d. 2001)
Poet Laureate, 1995-1997

James Still, novelist, short story writer, and poet was born on Double Branch Farm July 16, 1906 near LaFayette, Alabama. He died April 28, 2001. He was the oldest son of ten children (five boys, five girls) born to James Alexander and Lonie (Lindsey) Still. Still often said, "I was born in a cotton patch," since that was one of his earliest memories. Stories told while hoeing cotton led to an early awareness of the power of words.

He graduated from Lincoln Memorial University in Harrogate, Tennessee in 1929, studied under the agrarians at Vanderbilt University where he earned an MA degree in 1930, and received a degree in library science from the University of Illinois.

During the Great Depression, Still served as librarian of the Hindman Settlement School for six years. The only asphalt road in the county at that time ran from Hazard and ended at Troublesome creek in downtown Hindman. As part of his library duties, he ran a volunteer library-on-foot delivering books to four one-room schools from a carton he carried on his back. Since 1932, except for the period of time from March, 1942 until September, 1945 when he served as a sergeant in the Army Air Corps, he has been associated with the Settlement School in Knott County, Kentucky.

The *Virginia Quarterly Review* published Still's first poem in 1935 and his first short story appeared a year later. *Hounds on the Mountain* was issued in book format in 1937. His novel, *River of Earth* (1940), is a realistic and imaginative tale of Brack Baldridge, a mountain man who lives at the headwaters of the Kentucky River and makes his living by working in and out of the coal camps. The publication of this book helped establish Still as a major literary figure as well as a voice of Appalachia. *Time Magazine* called it "a work of art." The book is still in print and considered an American classic.

During the 1930s and '40s Still was routinely published in some of the nation's better known publications such as *The Atlantic* and *The Saturday Evening Post*. During the 1960's and into 70's his writing received little notice, mostly due to Still's reluctance to promote his own work. In 1976, following the publication by Gnomon Press of Still's collection of short stories, *Pattern of a Man*, his work was rediscovered. This was followed by a period of productive literary activity during the remaining years of Still's life.

Still is admired for his unadorned language which captures the essence of Appalachian speech and the human condition. His publications of poems, stories, and novels include *On Troublesome Creek* (1941), *Pattern of a Man* (1976), *Sporty Creek*, a novel (1977), *The Run for the Elbertas* (stories, 1980), and *The Wolfpen Notebooks: Appalachian Life* (1991), and *From the Mountain, From the Valley: New and Collected Poems* (2001).

Still's children's books include *Way Down Yonder on Troublesome Creek* (1974), *The Wolfpen Rusties* (1975), *Jack and the Wonder Beans* (1977), and his latest, *An Appalachian Mother Goose* (1998).

His awards are numerous— Two Guggenheim Fellowships in 1941 and 1946, the O. Henry Award for "Bat Flight" and again for "Proud Walkers," the American Academy of Arts and Letters Award and a National Institute of Arts and Letters Award in 1947. His stories have appeared in *Best American Short Stories* for 1946 and 1950; and *The American Tradition*, and *The Yale Review Anthology*. His biography appeared in *Who's Who in America, 2000*.

Still moved into a log house located on Little Carr Creek in 1939, intending to stay long enough to write his novel *River of Earth*. He continued to occupy the two-story house until his death, more than a half century later. [55, 56]

Memories stirred Still to create his book *An Appalachian Mother Goose*. "We all know about Jack and Jill, and that fateful trip up the hill, but whatever became of those clumsy kids?" [57]

Jill came to life, became Jack's wife,
And soon they had a daughter;
Jack spent his days in several ways,
The womenfolk fetched the water.

And do you want to know what
Little girls are really made of?
Buttons, bows, squeals and cries,
Tears and sighs and mud pies.

"Sometimes children, they come up and ask me 'How do you write a poem?' I finally decided on an answer. Ellen LeClark, who is Mrs. Rob Penn Warren, told me once what to do if I were attacked by an octopus . . . 'the only thing you can do is to reach in its mouth and get a handful of something and turn it wrong side out.' Now, that's what you do with a subject. You turn it wrong side out." [58]

HERITAGE

— From *The Wolfpen Poems* [59]

I shall not leave these prisoning hills
Though they topple their barren heads to level earth
And the forests slide uprooted out of the sky.
Through the waters of Troublesome, of Trace Fork,
Of Sand Lick rise in a single body to glean the valleys,
To drown lush pennyroyal, to unravel rail fences;
Through the sun-ball breaks the ridges into dust
And burns its strength into the blistered rock
I cannot leave. I cannot go away.
Being of these hills, being one with the fox
Stealing into the shadows, one with the new-born foal,
The lumbering ox drawing green beech logs to mill,
One with the destined feet of man climbing and descending
And one with death rising to bloom again, I cannot go.
Being of these hills I cannot pass beyond.

JOY BALE BOONE
(b. 1912 – d. 2002)
Poet Laureate, 1997-1999

Joy Bale Boone was born October 29, 1912, in Chicago to William Sydney and Edith Field. She was educated at the Chicago Latin School and the Roycemore School for Girls in Evanston, Illinois.

She lived in Elizabethtown for many years, raising six children and becoming active in Kentucky causes. Among the many stories she enjoyed telling were of the times as a young woman in Chicago when she met Harriet Monroe, editor of *Poetry*, and Al Capone, who "seemed to be a perfect gentleman."

She served on the Kentucky Council on Higher Education and the Friends of Kentucky Libraries board during the bookmobile years. After her husband, Garnet Bale died, she married George Street Boone and moved to Elkton, Kentucky. In her later years

71

she divided her time between homes in Elkton and Glasgow, Kentucky.

Boone first came to the attention of Kentucky literary circles in 1945 as a reviewer for the *Louisville Courier-Journal*. She edited two collections of *Contemporary Kentucky Poets* (1964, 1967), and in 1964, founded *Approaches*, a literary magazine which eventually evolved into the highly regarded *Kentucky Poetry Review*. Boone's long narrative poem *The Storm's Eye: A Narrative in Verse Celebrating Cassius Marcellus Clay, Man of Freedom 1810-1903*, was published in 1974 by the Kentucky Poetry Press and was reprinted in the tenth anniversary issue of *Approaches*. Her other works include: *never less than love* and *Even Without Love*. Boone once wrote, when asked how a poem is made, "I realized the poet is made more by the poem than the poem by the poet."

Joy served as president of Friends of Kentucky Libraries. She chaired the Robert Penn Warren Committee at Western Kentucky University beginning with its inception in 1987 and was instrumental in the establishment of the Robert Penn Warren Room and Library at WKU. Her awards include the Distinguished Kentuckian Award from Kentucky Education Television in 1974 and the Sullivan Award from the University of Kentucky in 1969.[60]

She is listed as a poet in *Who's Who of American Women*, and *Who's Who in the South and Southwest*. Her passion for poetry has led her down many paths: as poet, advocate, and editor. Joy was an example to all of us, exalting through her art the gift of life and the beauty and joy within.

Joy Boone's poem, "Prologue 1894," tells of the elderly Cassius Clay's marriage to Dora, the 15-year-old daughter of a Valley View tenant farmer.

PROLOGUE 1894
— from *The Storm's Eye* [61]

Close to the end of his flamboyant seasons,
seasons measured by decades,
ten bringing him to rare man's full estate,
he put November to the test,
high-heart beside his youthful bride.
No spring had ever brought the White Hall grounds
more sure renewal.
Warming the room where its small assemblage stood,
the glowing firewood evoked red roses for the bride.
      "Dora of Valley View, do you...?"
In a gentle voice
becoming her fifteen years,
she answered to her man's kind friend,
a mountaineer of staunch Kentucky clan
daring to say the rite for Cassius Clay.
Morning-wedded, love's hours not yet given,
Clay, Lion of White Hall,
maned in color of his manor's name,
faced the posse of a judge
who thought the rescue of an old man's bride
was righteousness suitable to the county.
Routed by Clay-manned cannon,
the seven men fell back,
blood marking their retreat,
red like broken petals from a bride's bouquet.
The startled men had no time to ask
      "Dora of Valley View, do you...?"

73

Gone were the slaves freed when Cassius heired
the great plantation,
and gone were servants banished by his grief
turned to suspicion:
only loud crickets of that wedding night gave song—
only two figures pleased the ballroom floor
and touched silver-silver of their cool goblets' rims;
only two turned from the empty room toward curving
          stairs
to claim pleasure and content within a canopied bed.
No shadows risked lurking by the wild cherry portal,
hand-carved and knobbed in coin, dulled by age.
          Dora Richardson Clay, you may
                    fill forty rooms and shaded maple groves
with joy and wonder to your simple taste,
lovely to him who seeks no old man's grace.

COLLECTED POEM

The final frustration
becomes the ultimate praise
of life.
We need
          No poem
          to hone.
No voice
to raise.

RICHARD LAWRENCE TAYLOR
(b. 1942)
Poet Laureate, 1999-2001

Richard Taylor is a professor of English at Kentucky State University in Frankfort. He holds a Ph.D. in English from the University of Kentucky and a JD from the University of Louisville as well as an MA in English.[62]

Taylor was born September 17, 1941 and grew up in Louisville. He and his wife live near Frankfort. They are the owners of Poor Richard's Bookstore in the historic section of downtown Frankfort.[63]

Among Taylor's works are *In the Country Morning Calm*, a book of poetry, and *Palisades of the Kentucky River*, co-published by the Kentucky Nature Conservancy along with scientists from the Kentucky State Nature Preserves Commission. Two collections of poems are *Bluegrass* and *Earth Bones*. He is also the author of *Girty*, a novel, and *Three Kentucky Tragedies*, part of the New Reader Series published by University Press of Kentucky.

In addition to his teaching and writing career, he has been active with the Governor's Scholars Program, the University Press of Kentucky editorial board, and the Kentucky Humanities Council speakers bureau. He has won two creative writing fellowships from the National Endowment for the Arts and an Al Smith Fellowship in Creative Writing from the Kentucky Arts Council.

Taylor's poem, "Upward Mobility" was selected as the top poem in the 1997 Jim Wayne Miller Prize in Poetry and appeared in *The Licking River Review*.

Taylor has received many grants and awards for both his writing and teaching of writing. Numerous stories and poems have been published in journals, chapbooks, and anthologies.

A POEM FOR LIZZ
— from *Earth Bones* [64]

Three times the butterfly,
a Diana Fritillary
with aqua ribbing on blue-black
hindwings,
circles and glides,
circles and lands
on the back of your outstretched hand.

The frail weave of its wings
knits and trembles
like fingers
on frets of a violin
a light candles through
their gauze.

Scaling the summit of your wrist,
it paused to test the wind,
anchored to that instant like stone.
Then both of you rise.

PREMISES
— from *Earth Bones* [65]

What we're looking for
is a place
with none of the conveniences.
Where the rocks
have not trimmed their nails.

Our needs are few
some bedrock, some water,
a view of the moon:
tadpoles swim in the print
of one hoof.

What we don't find
we'll scavenge and build.

We'll bring our own tools
and plant by the signs.

All we are asking is
a goldfinch in the chicory.

JAMES BAKER HALL
(b. 1935)
Poet Laureate, 2001-2003

James Baker Hall grew up in Lexington, Kentucky, where he was a multi-sport star athlete at Henry Clay High School. He has maintained an interest in sports throughout his life.

He graduated from the University of Kentucky in 1957, then received a Wallace Stegner Fellowship at Stanford University where he earned his masters degree in 1961. Hall has taught English at the University of Kentucky since 1973. He is married to fiction writer Mary Ann Taylor-Hall.

Hall is known not only as an author of fiction and poetry but also as an accomplished photographer.

He published his first book of poetry in 1975 and has authored five volumes of poetry, which include *Standing on the Edge to*

Wave, The Mother on the Other Side of the World and *Her Name.*[66] Hall also has written two novels and the text for photography books. He is a contributing editor for *Aperture.* Among the many magazines that have published his work are *The New Yorker, The Paris Review, Poetry, The American Poetry Review* and *The Kenyon Review.*

Published in 2001, *A Spring-Fed Pond* by Hall included nearly one hundred photographs of five of Hall's colleagues, including his wife Mary Ann Taylor-Hall, who is a prominent author in her own right. The book documented in photographs the maturation of authors Wendell Berry, Gurney Norman, Bobbie Ann Mason, Ed McClanahan and Taylor-Hall.

Hall received a 1979-80 National Endowment in the Arts grant for poetry, and has won awards from *Ironwood* and the *Cincinnati Poetry Review.* In addition to his teaching and writing career, he serves on the advisory board of the Kentucky Writers Coalition.[67]

In 1994 Hall received the prestigious Chancellor's Award for Outstanding Teaching in the Tenured Faculty at University of Kentucky. His most recent book is *Praeder's Letters: A Novel in Verse* (2002).

ARS POETICA
— from *The Mother on the Other Side of the World*[68]

the way a fox slips into one side
of your headlights and carrying his tail
(like a pen running out of ink) slips
out the other—

THE GATE
— from *The Mother on the Other Side of the World* [69]

would I have folded back the gate
would I have gotten down on my knees
would I have shut my eyes held my breath
would I have touched and stroked it
would I have tried to embrace it
would I have been able to imagine
anything else to do

THE BUFFALO
— from *The Mother on the Other Side of the World* [70]

crossing the yard to the old wall
I'm drawn along a circle
through each thing a full moon
seen over a considerable area of the earth
including the vast oceans rises
and walks down the wall
and through me
in the evolving white shape of cat
for years these stones lay afield
gathering his footsteps even the clicks
sound old and have come a long way
his fur slipping through my hands
what did my ancestor hear
upon seeing the Shawnee step into
this moonlight with a small stone taken up
and shaped to his use what did the Shawnee hear
when the gun was cocked where did the sounds go
when the buffalo were slaughtered

were they fixed in time
or were they freed
into the real world mistaken
for snapping twigs or distant
thunder or history at night
when the small creatures walk this wall
isn't it the same gravity audible
the weight of each thing settling
defining the size of its earth the dead
clicking along in the moonlight with us
great silence in between
and within each of them
the dwindling herds
thundering back and forth
far and then farther away
the dwindling gunshots and screams
we shot them from trains for sport
we ate their tongues

JOE SURVANT
Poet Laureate 2003-

photo by Ashley Survant

Joe Survant[71] grew up in Owensboro, Kentucky, on the Ohio River, hunting, fishing, camping and contracting a chronic love for rivers, woods, and damp bottoms where weeds "in wheels, shoot long and lovely and lush." When he was a senior in High School he met his wife, Jeannie Ashley, and along with his friend, science fiction writer Terry Bisson, started the first Literary Magazine at Owensboro High School.

Survant attended college at the University of Kentucky where he studied with creative writing teacher Robert Hazel. He had literature classes with Robert White and Bill Axton. These, along with friendships with classmates Lamar Herrin, Richard Taylor, and Louise Natcher Murphy, prompted him to change his major

82

from physics to English. By the time he was a senior he was writing madly and followed Richard Taylor as the editor of the campus literary magazine, *Stylus*.

In the early 1960s he attended the University of Delaware where he continued writing and twice won the Academy of American Poets Prize. After teaching at the University of Kentucky for a couple of years he returned to Delaware where he received the PhD degree in 1970. Since then he has been teaching writing and contemporary literature at Western Kentucky University. He lives with his wife in Warren County where their daughters, Anastasia and Alexandria were born.

During 1983-84 Survant spent a year at the Universiti Sains Malaysia in Penang on a Fulbright Fellowship. This period afforded him the time and opportunity to travel in SE Asia, as well as renew his interest in writing. He wrote every day and completed his first book, *In the Forest of Rain*. A portion of the manuscript titled *The Presence of Snow in the Tropics* was published in 2001. Upon his return to Bowling Green and Western Kentucky University in 1984, he was instrumental, along with Frank Steele and Mary Ellen Miller, in the establishment of a creative writing major at the school.

In the early 1990s, Survant says, he "tired of the lyric voice pacing the narrow room of its own consciousness." He began to experiment with joining the lyric to a narrative. He chose Kentucky's rural past as the subject matter for this form. His first result was a chapbook, *We Will All Be Changed,* which won a competition and was published by Judith Kitchen's State Street Press. The next year his book, *Anne & Alpheus, 1842-1882*, won the Arkansas Poetry Prize and was published by the University of Arkansas Press.

Anne & Alpheus became the first of a trilogy of narrative poem-novels. The second was *Rafting Rise,* a story of logging on the Rough, Green, and Ohio Rivers in the early 1900s. Survant has just begun a partial retirement, teaching only in the spring, and at this writing is at work on the third book of the Kentucky trilogy, tentatively titled *First West*.

THE GOLDEN CIRCUMSTANCE
— from *Rafting Rise* [72]

I saw autumn coming toward me
in a golden dress green hemmed
with scarlet petticoat. I looked
right through her and saw the old forest.

inside her trees. I looked and
I was she. I heard then the
ancient languages of elms about
to be forgotten and the words of men

already fallen from memory.
Around me the urgent voices
of sapling redbuds and sassafras
were like a choir of locusts. I felt

the dying maple blaze in the distance
and smelled the dark wet ashes
of the earth. I tasted winter in
my mouth like a strong lover.

Then I began to turn and dance
with my golden circumstance.

THE STONE
— from *The Presence of Snow in the Tropics* [73]

When you were born a tall handsome woman with the slenderest of fingers gave you back your stone. She placed it on your tongue like an aspirin and held your mouth shut and stroked your throat until you had to swallow. The stone is smooth, shaped and pressed by the weight of all the world's waters, rolled by the journeys of all the world's rivers to the sea. Inside you it becomes a perfect sphere the size of a pea. A thin layer of cells coats it so that you can carry it all your life like a shark carries souvenirs from all its meals.

When you are ready to die the woman will come again. She will still be handsome and her fingers will still be sharp. With incredible ease, and drawing very little blood, she will reach through your side and pluck out the stone, now big as a cherry. It has absorbed all your days and nights which give it the color of pale blood. It is your stone, but she will keep it for you. When she swallows the stone your heart will burst. When your are ready to try again, she will come to you. She will put the stone on your tongue and hold your mouth and stroke and stroke your throat. It will be harder to swallow. You will always wish for a smaller stone.

PART III

Scrapbook

House Resolution No. 16 designating Professor J.T.C. Noe as Poet Laureate of Kentucky.

CHAPTER 368

HOUSE RESOLUTION No. 16

Whereas, Kentuckians at all times have delighted to honor their men and women who have achieved distinction in any calling or profession, and

Whereas, Prof. J. T. C. Noe of the College of Education, University of Kentucky, is recognized by all who know him, who have read his poems, or been charmed by his literary productions, and is deserving of all the high commendations his friends and fellow citizens willingly shower upon him; therefore,

Be it resolved by the General Assembly of the Commonwealth of Kentucky:

That Prof. J. T. C. Noe is hereby declared to be the Poet Laureate of Kentucky and that he is privileged to enjoy all the honors incidental thereto. It is expressly understood, however, that this declaration of distinction is an honorary one only and bears with it no financial obligation upon the Commonwealth. This resolution shall become effective on and after is (its) passage by the Legislature and approval by the Governor.

Neither approved nor disapproved.

House Resolution No. 190 designating Lowell Allen Williams as
Poet Laureate of Kentucky

CHAPTER 190
(H. R. 5)

A JOINT RESOLUTION naming Lowell Allen Williams as Poet Laureate
of Kentucky.

WHEREAS, Lowell Allen Williams, a resident of Cunningham, Carlisle
county, Kentucky, has for more than twenty years been writing
poetry of such merit as to gain for him several prizes in poetry
contests; and

WHEREAS, Lowell Allen Williams has achieved great distinction by
having numerous volumes of his work published, by having numer-
ous poems published in national newspapers and magazines, and
broadcast over the radio; and

WHEREAS, Lowell Allen Williams has achieved great distinction by
receiving the enthusiastic recognition of many fellow poets and
writers, including Edgar A. Guest, the nationally famous poet, Hon-
orable Alben W. Barkley, Charles B. Driscoll, Fred G. Neuman and
other writers of note; and

WHEREAS, Lowell Allen Williams has been writing of Kentucky, its
people and customs for twenty years, and by his poetic works has
shown his warm understanding and appreciation of Kentucky and
its people;

NOW, THEREFORE,

*Be it resolved by the General Assembly of the Common-
wealth of Kentucky:*

Section 1. That Lowell Allen Williams is hereby declared
to be a poet laureate of Kentucky and that he is privileged to
enjoy all the honors incidental thereto. It is expressly under-
stood, however, that this declaration of distiction is an honorary
one only and bears with it no financial obligation upon the
Commonwealth of Kentucky.

Section 2. That the Secretary of State be, and she hereby
is directed to forward a copy of this Resolution, properly attested
under the Seal of the Commonwealth of Kentucky, and a suitable
commission, also properly attested, to Lowell Allen Williams
declaring him to be Poet Laureate of Kentucky.

Approved February 27, 1956

Joint Resolution, S.R. 10 designating Jesse Hilton Stuart and Edwin Carlisle Litsey as Poets Laureate of Kentucky.

CHAPTER 251
(S. R. 10)

A JOINT RESOLUTION naming Jesse Hilton Stuart and Edwin Carlile Litsey as Poets Laureate of Kentucky.

WHEREAS, the death of the Poet Laureate, the beloved J. T. Cotton Noe, has left Kentucky in need of one who truly represents its great spirit and traditions, and

WHEREAS, the people of Kentucky desire to honor their men and women who have achieved distinction in any calling or profession, and

WHEREAS, there now resides within Kentucky two native sons, Jesse Hilton Stuart and Edwin Carlile Litsey, who are known and recognized throughout the nation as writers and poets of eminent distinction, and

WHEREAS, Jesse Hilton Stuart has written many short stories, novels such as "Taps for Private Tussie" and "The Good Spirit of Laurel Ridge", and the volumes of poetry, "Man With A Bull-Tongue Plow", "Album of Destiny" and "Kentucky Is My Land", and

WHEREAS, Jesse Hilton Stuart was awarded the Guggenheim fellowship for European travel in 1937; the Jeanette Sewal Davis poetry prize in 1934; a prize from the Academy of Arts and Sciences in 1941 and the Thomas Jefferson Southern Award in 1943, and

WHEREAS, Edwin Carlile Litsey, a resident of Lebanon, Marion county, Kentucky has for more than sixty years been writing poetry of such merit as to gain for him five prizes in nationwide poetry contests; and

WHEREAS, Edwin Carlile Litsey has achieved great distinction by having twelve volumes of his work published, by having his work published in numerous magazines and broadcast over the radio; and

WHEREAS, Edwin Carlile Litsey is a Life Member of The Academic Society of International History of Paris, France, of The Arts Club of New York and of The Authors Club of London, England; and

WHEREAS, both Jesse Hilton Stuart and Edwin Carlile Litsey, in their devoted and enthusiastic services to the Commonwealth, have shown the greatest understanding and appreciation of Kentucky and her people and have brought honor and glory to the Commonwealth of Kentucky,

NOW, THEREFORE,

Be it resolved by the General Assembly of the Commonwealth of Kentucky:

Section 1. That Jesse Hilton Stuart and Edwin Carlile Litsey are hereby declared to be the Poets Laureate of Kentucky and each is entitled to enjoy all the honors incidental thereto. This declaration of distinction, however, is honorary only and bears no financial obligation upon the Commonwealth of Kentucky.

Section 2. That the Secretary of State be, and he hereby is, directed to forward copies of this resolution, properly attested under the seal of the Commonwealth of Kentucky, and suitable commissions, also properly attested, to Jesse Hilton Stuart and Edwin Carlile Litsey declaring each to be a Poet Laureate of Kentucky.

Approved March 22, 1954

James Still's letter in response to a request for biographical information for this book:

Feb. 9, 1999

Betty,
You have set quite a task for a man aged 92½. This copy of my bio in forthcoming Who's Who in America will have to serve — in the 2000 edition. What a curious undertaking. One Poet Laureate told me he never wrote a poem in his life, only fishing articles. How does it happen Wendell Berry was not lately chosen?
Yes Mary Ellen Miller was Jim Wayne's wife.
I'm not about to start writing about myself. Yet. King Library Editions (U.K.) has just published (privately, limited ed.) a story of my childhood — in my own words. (Wade Hall's words, mostly.)

Truly,
James Still

My new book, say they, is doing well. About time some one took on Mother Goose.
April 15, a dramatized version of my Jack and Wonder Beans to be performed in new History Building (Frankfort) 7:00 PM.

92

The text of James Still's letter in response to a request for biographical information for this book:

Feb. 9, 1999

Betty,

    You have set quite a task for
a man aged 92½. This copy of my
bio in forthcoming *Who's Who in America*
will have to serve – in the 2000 edition.

    What a curious undertaking. One
Poet Laureate told me he never wrote
a poem in his life, only fishing articles.

    How does it happen Wendell
Berry was not lately chosen?

    Yes Mary Ellen Miller was
Jim Wayne's wife.

    I'm not about to start writing
about myself. Yet. King Library
Editions (U.K.) has just published
(privately, limited ed.) a story
of my childhood – in my own
words. (Wade Hall's words, mostly.)

        Truly,
        James Still

My new book, say they, is doing
well. About time some one took
on Mother Goose.

    April 15, a dramatized version
of my *Jack and Wonder Beans*
to be performed in new History Building
(Frankfort) 7:00 PM.

In 1939 James Still moved into this log house between Dead Mare Branch and Wolfpen Creek, intending to stay long enough to complete his novel, *River of Earth*. He occupied the house for the rest of his life.

James Still in his log house. August of 1990 during a tour by participants in the Appalachian Writers' Workshop at the Hindman Settlement School.

James Still cutting flowers
in the yard of his log
house, August 1990.

Verna Mae Sloan, Joy Bale Boone, and James Still, August 1990,
during the Appalachian Writers' Workshop.

The W-Hollow homeplace of Jesse, James, and Mary Stuart.
The log house is over 120 years old. Mary is sitting in the rocking
chair on the porch on her birthday August 6, 1999.

Lee Pennington, speaker at the Kentucky State Poetry Society
Awards Banquet at the Jesse Stuart Lodge, Greenbo Lake State
Park, 1998.

The Marion National Bank of Lebanon with which Edward Litsey
was associated for more than seventy years.

Jim Wayne Miller lecturing at the Appalachian Writers' Workshop, August 1990.

Paul Salyers at the Flatwoods Poetry Society's 30th Founder's Day with friends Camila Haney and Bill Justice on the left.

Lela Mae Pilkenton, widow of Henry Pilkenton. October 2000, Elizabethtown Kentucky.

Left to right: Governor Paul Patton, Joy Bale Boone, and Richard
Taylor. On the occasion of Taylor's installation as Poet Laureate.
Boone is the out-going Poet Laureate.

Frankfort, April 24, 2001: On the occasion of the induction of
James Baker Hall as Poet Laureate. Left to right: Crystal
Wilkinson, Richard Taylor, Governor Paul Patton, James Baker
Hall, Gerri Combs, Frank X Walker.

PART IV

Bibliography

Across the Wide, Green Valley, Poems of America Series III, by Lowell Allen Williams, preface and introduction, Simons Historical Publication, Melber, Kentucky, 1991.

A Literary History of Kentucky, William S. Ward, with foreword by Thomas D. Clark, 1988. The University of Tennessee Press, Knoxville, first edition.

A Literary History of Kentucky, William S. Ward, p 339.

A World of Books, by Lillie D. Chaffin with R. Conrad Stein, Chicago, Children's Press, 1970.

Appalachian Express, Pikeville, Kentucky, from the Clipping Division of Kentucky Press Service, Inc., 63 Fountain Place, Frankfort, Kentucky, 40601; Dec. 22, 1979, "Kentucky Has Three Poet Laureates."

The Blue Moon, a bimonthly publication of the Kentucky Arts Council, Vol. 8, Issue 2, March/April, 2001.

Copperhead Cane, Poems by Jim Wayne Miller, introduction, 1995, Green River Writers, Grex Press, Louisville, Kentucky.

Contemporary Authors, Vol. 69-72, Gale Research Company, Book Tower, Detroit, Michigan 48226, 1978.

Contemporary Authors, New Revision Series, Vol. 20, p 339, IBID p 308.

Earth Bones, Richard Taylor, "A Poem for Liz," "Premises" *Frankfort State Journal*, Jan. 13, 1980, Rick Zurcher.

History of Kentucky, The Bluegrass State, Volume III. The S.J. Clarke Publishing Company, Chicago-Louisville, 1928.

Journal of the Senate of the General Assembly of the Commonwealth of Kentucky, Regular Session of 1976, March 11, 1976.

Kentucky Authors, 175th Anniversary Edition, Sister Mary Carmel Browning, Ohio State University, Printed by Keller-Crescent Co., Evansville, Indiana, 1968.

Kentucky Literature (1900-1950), William Rouse Jillson, Frankfort, Kentucky, 1956.

Kentucky Poet Laureates, The Department of Education and The Department of Libraries and Archives, Frankfort, Kentucky.

Memories, Moods, and Meditations, pp 55-56, by Henry E. Pilkenton.

Morehead Statement, A Quarterly Publication for Alumni and Other Friends of Morehead State University, Summer 1995, Vol. 19, No 1.

Obituary, Litsey, Special to the *Courier-Journal*, Louisville, Kentucky, Feb. 1970.

Poet Laureates of Britain: Lincoln Library of Essential Information, The Frontier Press Company, Buffalo, New York, 1938.

The Daily Independent, Today's Living, "Mother Goose Meets the Hills, Appalachian Memories stir James Still to create book" by Allen Breed, The Associated Press, Oct. 11, 1998 edition, p 25, Ashland, Kentucky.

The Franklin Favorite, Dec. 1, 1988 edition, "A Slice of Life, the rhyme of reason," by Jill E. Brown, IBID, Brown.

The Hardin County Independent, March 5, 1998, "Golden Poet, Golden Words" by Bob Villanueva.

The Jesse Stuart Foundation, 1645 Winchester Avenue, Ashland, Kentucky 41105, James M. Gifford, executive director.

The Kentucky Encyclopedia, The University Press of Kentucky, 1992, Jim Wayne Miller, pp 855-856.

The Kentucky Encyclopedia, ed. John E. Kleiber, The University Press of Kentucky, 1992, p 98 by Mary Ellen Miller.

The Kentucky Poet Laureate Post 1991: The Kentucky General Assembly KRS 153.600.

The Lebanon Enterprise "In his own write, Kentucky poet laureate Edwin Carlisle Litsey was an individualist from the first word," by Terry Ward.

The Lexington-Herald Leader, Maurice Manning, "The Storm's Eye" by Joy Bale Boone, "Prologue" pp 1-2.

The Shadow Voice, Edward G. Hill, 1928, The Standard Printing Company, Inc., Louisville, Kentucky.

Somewhere in the Schemes, Poems by Jim Patton, Jr., p 18.

The Time Almanac, 1999, Borgna Brunner, editor, "Poet Laureates of the United States."

"Trout's Trotline: Kentucky's in Truly Sad Shape—It Boasts Nary a Poet Laureate: So Here Are Two Likely Candidates," Allen M. Trout, *Courier-Journal*, Frankfort Bureau, Dec. 27, 1953.

World Book Encyclopedia, 1982, Chicago, Illinois, "Origination of Poet Laureates."

The Wolfpen Poems, James Still, "Heritage," p 82.

PART V

References and notes:

[1] *The Penguin Dictionary of Literary Theory*, third edition, J.A. Cuddon, 1976-1991, p 725-726, Penguin Books USA, Inc., Hudson Street, New York, NY 10014.

[2] *The New Encyclopedia Britannica*, Vol. 9, 15th ed., 1997, p 542.

[3] *The Kentucky Encyclopedia*, John E. Kleber, Editor in Chief, University Press of Kentucky, 1992. p. 683.

[4] William Rouse Jillson, *Kentucky Literature*, (1900-1950), Frankfort; Roberts Printing Company, 1956 p. 100.

[5] Sister Mary Carmel Browning, Ohio State University, *Kentucky Authors*, 175th Anniversary Edition, Keller-Crescent Printing Company, Evansville, Indiana, 1968. p. 60.

[6] *Louisville Herald-Post*, July 6, 1930

[7] Kentucky Department for Libraries and Archives Public Records Division Archival Services Branch, Frankfort, Kentucky.

[8] Information provided by Pat Wicker of Kuttawa, a niece by marriage of Louise Scott Phillips. Picture provided by Frances Houghland, Paducah, Kentucky.

[9] *The Kentucky Encyclopedia*, editor John E. Kleiber, The University Press of Kentucky, 1992, p. 562.

[10] Special to the *Courier-Journal*, 1970, Louisville, KY, obituary.

[11] *The Kentucky Encyclopedia*, John E. Kleber, Editor in Chief, University Press of Kentucky, 1992. p. 563. Wade Hall was a close friend of Litsey's according to Litsey's cousin Elizabeth Litsey Hagan of Springfield, KY, April 10, 2001.

[12] Photo supplied by Jesse Stuart's sister, Mary Stuart Nelson.

[13] Dr. James Gifford, executive director of the Jesse Stuart Foundation in Ashland, KY, writes a regular column about Stuart for the local newspaper, *The Independent*, which helps to keep the legacy of Stuart alive. The foundation has become a regional press and bookseller. Much of the following information comes directly from an article in the *Sunday Independent*, June 28, 1998 titled "Foundation Preserves Legacy of Jesse Stuart." For more information about Stuart and the foundation write The Jesse Stuart Foundation, 1645

Winchester Avenue, P.O. Box 669, Ashland, KY 41105 or call
(606) 326-1667 or (606) 326-1487.

[14] Ibid.

[15] *The Kentucky Encyclopedia*, John E. Kleber, Editor in Chief,
University Press of Kentucky, 1992. Jerry Herndon, p. 858-859.
Also see Harold E. Richardson, *Jesse, The Biography of an
American Writer, Jesse Hilton Stuart* (New York 1984) and Ruel
E. Foster, *Jesse Stuart* (New York 1968).

[16] *Kentucky Authors*, 175th Anniversary Edition, Sister Mary Carmel
Browning. Ohio State University, Evansville, IN, 1968, p. 65-76.

[17] Ibid.

[18] Ibid.

[19] New York: E.P. Dutton, 1934

[20] Jesse Stuart Foundation, 1988

[21] *Louisville Courier-Journal*, Allen M. Trout, "Trout's Trotlines,"
"Kentucky's Poet Laureate," 1956

[22] *Across the Wide, Green Valley, Poems of America, Series III*, by
Lowell Allen Williams, preface and introduction, Simons
Historical Publication, Melber, KY, 1991.

[23] Photograph supplied by Robert W. Witt, editor, *The Chaffin Journal*.

[24] *A World of Books*, by Lillie D. Chaffin with R. Conrad Stein, Chicago,
Children's Press, 1970. p 12-13, 32, 40-41.

[25] *Morehead Statement*, a quarterly publication for alumni and friends of
Morehead State University, Summer, 1995, Vol. 19, No. 1.

[26] "Observation" is quoted from *A Stone for Sisyphus*, published by South
and West, Inc., Fort Smith, Arkansas.

[27] "No Praise for Once" is quoted from *A Stone for Sisyphus*, published
by South and West, Inc., Fort Smith, Arkansas.

[28] Information supplied by son Randy Mobley of Louisville, KY and
daughter, Mary Chase Mobley of Grand Rapids, MI.

[29] The *Courier-Journal*, "Thomas L. Mobley, former state senator from
Jefferson, dies," October 20, 1996, obituary, p 11B, metro edition.

[30] *Journal of the Senate of the General Assembly of the Commonwealth
of Kentucky*, Regular Session of 1976, March 11, 1976.

[31] personal communications.

[32] Photo of Agnes O'Rear on her seventieth birthday at her daughter's
home in Frankfort, KY, 1965.

[33] *Frankfort State Journal*, January 13, 1980, Rick Zurcher.

[34] Ibid.

[35] Annotations for "Autobiography" supplied by O'Rear's daughter, Mrs. V.O. Barnard, Jr., (Jinks O'Rear Barnard).

[36] All biographical information was provided by Soc Clay.

[37] *Contemporary Authors*, Vol. 69-72, Gale Research Company, Book Tower, Detroit, MI, 48226, 1978.

[38] Ibid. p 337.

[39] "Poet of the Flowers" is from Lee Pennington's book *Songs of Bloody Harlan*, 1971 & 1975. Westburg Association, Fennimore, Wisconsin. Pennington says it's one of his favorite poems and is included here at his request.

[40] Louisville, Ky. Green River Writers/Grex Press, 1993

[41] Hazel F. Goddard, editor, *Amber Magazine*, Nova Scotia.

[42] Information and poems provided by Paul Salyers.

[43] Information and photo provided by Dale Faughn.

[44] *Contemporary Authors*, New Revision Series, Vol. 20, p. 339.

[45] Ibid. p. 308.

[46] *A Literary History of Kentucky*, William S. Ward, p 339.

[47] *Copperhead Cane, Poems by Jim Wayne Miller*, Introduction, Green River Writers/Grex Press, Louisville, Ky, 1995

[48] Nashville, Tennessee: Robert Moore Allen, 1964, and a reprint: Louisville, Ky. Green River Writers/Grex Press, 1995

[49] Information supplied by Henry E. Pilkenton's daughter, Emily S. Bogard.

[50] "Golden Poets, Golden Words," by Bob Villleanueva, the *Hardin County Independent*, March 5, 1998.

[51] *The Franklin Favorite*, Thursday, December 1, 1998, "A Slice of Life," The Rhyme of Reason, by Jill E. Brown.

[52] Ibid.

[53] *Somewhere in the Scheme*, Poems by Jim Patton, Jr.

[54] Ibid. (Patton, in this book, wrote several different poems entitled "At Seven.")

[55] *The Kentucky Encyclopedia*, editor John E. Kleiber, The University Press of Kentucky, 1992, Jim Wayne Miller, p 855-856.

[56] Lexington, Kentucky: University Press of Kentucky. *From the Mountain, From the Valley*, ed. Ted Olson. "A Man Singing to Himself: An Autobiographical Essay" by James Still.

[57] *The Sunday Independent*, Today's Living "Mother Goose Meets the Hills, Appalachian Memories stir James Still to create book" by Allen Breed. The Associated Press, Sunday, October 11, 1998, p 25. Ashland, KY.

[58] "Still's Love of Life Reflected in Novels and Poetry," *All Things Considered* (National Public Radio), 11-10-1995.

[59] Berea, Ky. Berea College Press, 1986

[60] *The Kentucky Encyclopedia*, edited by John E. Kleiber, The University Press of Kentucky, 1992. p 98, by Mary Ellen Miller.

[61] Louisville, Ky. Kentucky Poetry Press

[62] From the 1999-2000 Kentucky Poet Laureate Nomination form biography. Taylor was nominated by the Kentucky Writers Coalition.

[63] Information provided by Richard Lawrence Taylor, professor of English, Kentucky State University.

[64] "A Poem for Lizz" by Richard Taylor is reprinted from the book *Earth Bones* by permission of Gnomon Press.

[65] "Premises" by Richard Taylor is reprinted from the book *Earth Bones* by permission of Gnomon Press.

[66] "Review for *The Mother on the Other Side of the World*" by Maurice Manning in the *Lexington-Herald Leader*, internet, http://www.sarabandebooks.org/sie/students/jbhr.html June 2, 2001.

[67] *The Blue Moon*, a bimonthly publication of the Kentucky Arts Council, Vol. 8, Issue 2, March/April, 2001.

[68] Reprinted from *The Mother on the Other Side of the World* by permission of Sarabande Books and James Baker Hall.

[69] Ibid.

[70] Ibid.

[71] Biographical information supplied by Joe Survant

[72] University Press of Florida, 2002. Reprinted by permission of Joe Survant.

[73] Landmark Books, 2001. Reprinted by permission of Joe Survant.